Theme park science

MARVELLOUS MACHINERY

By Nathan Lepora

ticktock

First published in Great Britain in 2008 by ticktock Media Ltd,
The Old Sawmill, 103 Goods Station Road, Tunbridge Wells, Kent.

ticktock project editor: Sophie Furse
ticktock picture researcher: Lizzie Knowles
ticktock project designer: Hayley Terry
With thanks to: Carol Ryback, Suzy Gazlay and Justin Spain

ISBN 978 1 84696 615 6 pbk

Printed in China
9 8 7 6 5 4 3
A CIP catalogue record for this book is available from the British Library.

Picture credits (t=top; b=bottom; c=centre; l=left; r=right):
Richard Bannister: 12, 13, 17b, 18, 29. Cedar Point: 2, 15, 28l. Imagebroker/ Alamy: 1. Interactive Rides, Inc. USA: 11t. Joel Rogers/ CoasterGallery.com: 16, 17t, 19b. www.coasterimage.com: 19. Shenval/ Alamy: 20. Shutterstock: OFC, 3, 4/5, 6/7 main, 6t, 8, 9, 21, 22, 23, 25t, OBCtr x2. Superstock: 24. John Taylor/ Alamy: 10/11 main. Wikipedia: 28r. www.coastersandmore.de: 26/27 main, 27 inset.

CONTENTS

CHAPTER 1: MACHINES

How would you describe a roller coaster? You could mention the amazing speed, the dizzying heights, and the exciting twists and turns. But basically, a roller coaster is a machine.

AMAZING MACHINES

Machines are all around us. We use them every day. Some are simple and some are complex. Wheelbarrows, scissors, and bottle openers are simple machines.

Complex machines include mechanical watches, cars, and jet airplanes.

THAT'S AMAZING!

Your muscles and bones form a natural machine – your body! This allows you to move.

A simple machine has one of four basic components: wheel, **ramp**, **pulley**, and **lever**. All machines contain at least one of these things. While most machines are tools that make our lives easier, some machines are built just for fun – like roller coasters.

A loop-the-loop on a roller coaster. The wheels and track are parts of an exciting machine.

WHAT IS A MACHINE?

A machine is a device that acts on another object. It might help you push or move something. People use machines to make a task easier. For example, a bicycle lets you move quickly with little effort.

The axle goes through the centre of this big wheel. The wheel rotates around the axle and is a simple machine.

SIMPLE AND COMPLEX MACHINES

A bottle opener is a very simple machine. It has no moving parts. Most machines, though, have many moving parts. The parts of a machine interact with each other to do work.

Kumba, at Superland, Israel has over 1,000 riders every hour.

A complex machine such as a theme park ride often contains a number of smaller, simple machines. For example, an engine may contain many moving parts that act as wheels and levers. These simple machines make the engine run.

DID YOU KNOW?

The world's first tubular steel roller coaster was **Matterhorn Bobsleds** in Disneyland, California, USA. It opened in 1959 and Walt Disney had the idea after a trip he made to the Swiss Alps.

CHAPTER 2: WHEELS AND RAMPS

Roller coasters use two basic types of simple machines – wheels and ramps. Wheels make the cars move. Ramps help the cars gain or lose height.

WHAT ARE WHEELS AND RAMPS?

Our everyday lives depend upon the wheel. Without it, we would have no easy way to transport objects or ourselves around. A wheel turning around a fixed **axle** is a simple machine.

A ramp is another simple and useful machine. We use ramps all the time without realising it.

Roller coasters are machines made of ramps and wheels

Pushing or pulling force

Ramp

A ramp is simply a slope, or **inclined plane**. Ramps allow us to raise or lower objects more easily.

THE ROLLER COASTER MACHINE

With some help from **gravity** and other **forces**, roller coasters deliver a thrilling ride! Gravity pulls all objects toward Earth. The force of gravity also makes objects accelerate (speed up), as they fall to the ground.

Gravity is about to pull this roller coaster down a slope. Its wheels allow a smooth ride at super-fast speeds.

THAT'S AMAZING!

Roller coasters have a set of wheels that fit below the tracks. These help to keep the car on the tracks, even when it's upside down!

Pulleys and levers are two types of simple machines. **Pulleys** change the direction in which a force pulls. **Levers** use a **pivot** point to help move an object. A seesaw is a common example of a lever.

WHAT IS A PULLEY?

A wheel and rope make up a simple machine called a pulley. The rope loops around the wheel to make it turn. Pulling one end of the rope turns the wheel. This pulls on an object attached to the other end of the rope. Some roller coasters use pulleys to pull the cars up the first hill.

Pulling down on one end of the rope lifts up the weight on the other end of the rope

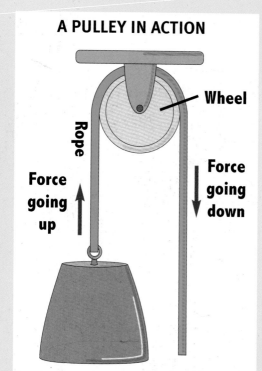

A PULLEY IN ACTION

Wheel

Rope

Force going up

Force going down

THAT'S AMAZING!

X-scream in Las Vegas, USA, is a seesaw ride over the edge of the Stratosphere Tower!

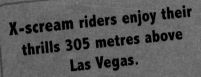

X-scream riders enjoy their thrills 305 metres above Las Vegas.

WHAT IS A LEVER?

A lever is a long bar that uses a pivot point. As one end is pushed down, the other end gets pushed up. The pivot point of a lever is not always in the middle. It can be at any point along the bar, including at either end.

PIVOT IN THE CENTRE OF LEVER

The weight of the two children pushes up the child at the other end.

PIVOT OFF-CENTRE

By moving the pivot point, the weight of one child is enough to push up the heavier weight of two children.

There are two ways to propel, or move, a roller coaster. One way is to pull it to the top of a hill. Another way is to **catapult** it into motion from standing still.

GRAVITATIONAL PROPULSION

Many roller coasters use gravity to propel them. A **chain lift** pulls the cars to the top of the first – and tallest – **lift hill**. Then gravity takes over. The **weight** of the cars helps pull the cars down, and the fun begins!

ROLLER COASTERS AND AUTOMOBILES

Roller coaster cars and automobiles can both travel fast, but they are propelled in very different ways. Automobiles have engines that provide power. Roller coaster cars have no engine. They cannot move by themselves. A separate source of power must propel a roller coaster car.

The roller coaster is pulled up the lift hill to the top . . .

. . . then gravity propels it down
the hill and through the ride.

Oblivion, a drop roller
coaster at Alton Towers in
Staffordshire, UK.

THAT'S AMAZING!

Oblivion plunges riders 60 metres
down an almost vertical drop at
speeds of 110 kilometres per hour.

LAUNCHED COASTERS

Some modern roller coasters are not pulled up a lift hill to be released. They are launched from the starting station, often shooting straight up a hill. These are called launched coasters.

MAGNETIC PROPULSION

One type of launch system uses **magnetic propulsion**. It works by using huge **electromagnets** fitted into the tracks and beneath the cars. It then changes the magnetic **poles** quickly to **attract** and **repel** the cars. This accelerates the cars around the tracks. **Wicked Twister** at Cedar Point is one roller coaster that uses this type of propulsion.

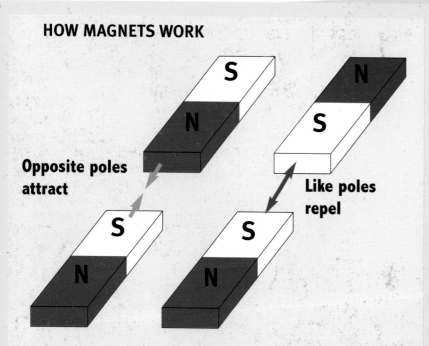

HOW MAGNETS WORK

Opposite poles attract

Like poles repel

If the car's magnets are N (North) and the track's magnets are S (South) they will be attracted (pulled together).

If the cars' magnets are N (North) and the track's magnets are also N (North) then they will be repelled (pushed apart).

The launch starts with the magnets on the track changing their poles to those opposite the car's magnets. For example, the cars are South so the track becomes North. This attracts the cars forward. Then, once the cars reach that set of magnets, they change poles, repelling the cars toward the next set of magnets.

THAT'S AMAZING!

Each time **Wicked Twister** passes through the station, it gets another boost of power. This means it gets faster and faster!

As the cars are repelled forward, the next set of magnets change their poles to attract the cars. This causes the cars to **accelerate**. This sequence continues until the train reaches its maximum speed.

Wicked Twister at Cedar Point, Ohio, USA. It shoots 65.5 metres into the air while twisting round and round.

Roller coasters have frames made either of wood or steel. Each material provides a thrilling but unique ride. Wood and steel frames react differently as the roller coaster cars roar over them.

WOODEN ROLLER COASTERS

Roller coaster builders have used wood frames for more than one hundred years. Wooden beams bolted together form a strong but flexible framework.

The wooden roller coaster **Son of Beast** in Ohio, USA is made from half a million metres of wood.

THAT'S AMAZING!

Son of Beast is the world's tallest wooden roller coaster. It is 66 metres high.

Son of Beast at Kings Island Amusement Park, Ohio, USA.

PROPERTIES OF WOOD

Wood is a great material for roller coaster structures. It is lighter than steel but still quite strong. It flexes (bends) and sways slightly as the cars roll along. Wooden-framed roller coasters rattle and shake. Many roller coaster fans enjoy this feeling!

STEEL ROLLER COASTERS

Many roller coaster frames are now built completely from steel. Their tracks are steel tubes joined to steel supports. This design allows for a smoother ride. Unlike wood, the steel frame does not move as the riders fly through incredible twists and loop-the-loops.

DID YOU KNOW?

A typical steel roller coaster like **The Big One** in Blackpool, UK, contains 2,215 tonnes of steel. Sixty thousand bolts hold it together.

From 1994-1996 The Big One was the world's fastest roller coaster at 140 kilometres per hour. It lost its record to Fujiyama in Japan.

The use of steel in roller coasters allows amazing designs. Cars can loop-the-loop many times or twist around and around. Some rides even zoom along upside-down or have rotating seats.

The Incredible Hulk at Universal Studios' Islands of Adventure, Orlando, USA.

PROPERTIES OF STEEL

Steel is an ideal material for building roller coasters. It is very strong and can be moulded into any shape. Long, curving sections welded together form **rigid** structures to provide a ride with sharp twists and turns.

The structure that supports a roller coaster is built using common construction methods. It consists of a series of vertical, horizontal, and crossbeam supports.

FANTASTIC FRAMEWORKS

Wooden roller coaster frames have **intricate** designs. Vertical (up-and-down) supports hold up the tracks. In between them, a lattice (an open pattern) of sideways and diagonal crossbeams strengthen the structure.

SUPPORTING LOADS

The load on a structure is the force that it must withstand without breaking. Most structures only need to support the weight of their materials. Roller coaster frameworks must also withstand additional forces as riders and cars thunder around the tracks.

Vertical support

Horizontal support

Crossbeam support

The intricate framework of a wooden roller coaster

Strong frameworks also support skyscrapers and other tall buildings. The Eiffel Tower in Paris, France, is a good example of a supporting lattice design.

The delicate-looking Eiffel Tower in Paris, France, has a strong framework. This means it can support its weight of 10,000 tonnes.

THAT'S AMAZING!

The Eiffel Tower in Paris, France, contains more than 18,000 iron beams and stretches 324 metres high.

THAT'S AMAZING!

The Spaceship Earth dome at The Epcot Centre, Florida, USA is a shape called **a geodesic dome.** It is very strong.

Spaceship Earth at Epcot at Walt Disney World, Florida, USA is made from 11,324 triangles.

STRONG SHAPES

Look at a roller coaster's frame. You can see that the crossbeams and supports often form triangles. Engineers use the triangle design because it is a very strong shape. If you push downward or sideways on a triangle, it keeps its shape.

A square is a weak shape compared to a triangle. A sideways force pushing on a square will usually squash it flat. A diagonal support or crossbeam strengthens a square shape because the square has become two triangles!

It is easy to see the triangles in this roller coaster frame

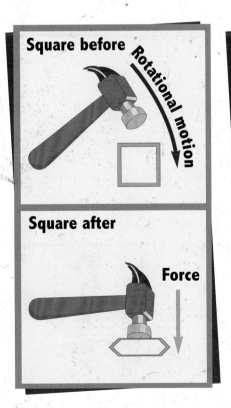

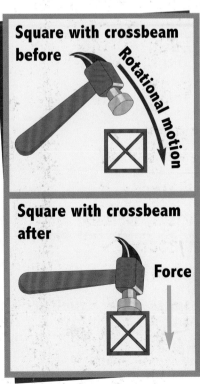

STEEL STRUCTURES

Like a triangle, a tube is another strong shape used in construction. The tube shape also helps to reduce the weight of the material. So instead of solid steel pipes, a roller coaster frame is often made of hollow steel tubes.

Some roller coaster riders prefer smooth rides. Others seek out a jolting, edge-of-their seats experience. Design engineers create their roller coaster layouts to give riders the maximum thrills. Every roller coaster has its own unique design.

The roller coaster Typhoon under construction in Lichtaart, Belgium.

DID YOU KNOW?

Most roller coasters are designed using a computer. That way, the designers can take 'virtual rides' themselves!

DESIGNED TO THRILL

Designers must think about who will ride their machine. Roller coasters designed for small children should have gentle hills and slow cars. Thrill seekers (like you!) prefer dizzying heights, sharp turns, and incredible speeds.

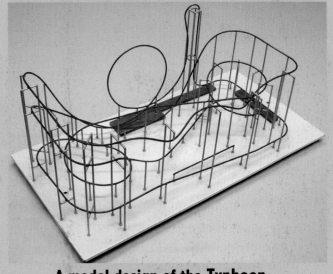

A model design of the Typhoon. This was made before the building work began.

The designers know exactly how to make their rides more exciting. The first drop is usually the steepest and most terrifying. It catches riders by surprise. Low 'head chopper' bars are another scary design trick. They are placed so it seems they just miss hitting riders' heads.

Future roller coasters could be taller than some skyscrapers. Others may have cars that magnetically hover above the tracks. Ideas from science fiction are rapidly becoming reality!

HIGH-TECH ADVANCES

Technology is advancing at a dizzying rate. High-tech materials are stronger and lighter than ever before. For example, the bodies of some modern cars are made from lightweight plastic **composites**. Cars made from these materials weigh less, which allows them to travel faster.

Riders on Millennium Force at Cedar Point, USA. It was the first roller coaster taller than 91 metres.

FUTURE ROLLER COASTERS

Roller coaster fans welcome all these advances in technology. They mean that every year, the rides become faster and more exciting!

For example, roller coasters keep getting taller. In 2000, Cedar Point in Ohio, USA built **Millennium Force**. It was the first 90 metre gigacoaster. Then in 2003, Cedar Point built **Top Thrill Dragster**. It was the first 120 metre stratocoaster.

The first stratocoaster, Top Thrill Dragster at Cedar Point, USA.

DID YOU KNOW?

The name for a 150 metre roller coaster has not yet been decided. Possible choices are 'atmocoaster' and 'teracoaster.'

Acceleration is a change in speed as time passes. An object that is gaining speed is accelerating. An object whose speed is decreasing is decelerating.

Attract means a force that pulls objects together. *(see also repel)*

Axle is the central rod around which a wheel turns.

Catapults are devices that launch a roller coaster ride from its starting point to an almost immediate high speed.

Chain lift is a device used to pull a roller coaster up a tall hill. It then releases the cars to accelerate down the other side of the hill. *(see also lift hill)*

Composite is something made up of two or more other materials.

Compressed air is air that is pressed into less space. It can be used to propel roller coasters into very fast launches.

Electromagnet is a magnet that produces a powerful magnetic force when electricity flows through it. *(see also magnets)*

Energy is the ability to make something happen. There are many forms of energy.

Force is a push or pull that changes the shape, speed, or direction of an object.

Geodesic dome is a domelike structure made from polygons (many-sided shapes) joined together. Triangles are often used because they are such strong shapes.

Gravity is the force that pulls one mass toward another. Gravity also causes falling objects to accelerate as they fall toward Earth.

Inclined plane is another name for a ramp. *(see also ramp)*

Intricate means complicated. The framework of the Eiffel Tower is made up of thousands of intricate lattice patterns which give the Tower its strength.

Kinetic energy is a type of energy from movement.

Lever is a simple machine made from a bar located over a pivot point. When one end of the bar is pushed down, the other end is pushed up.

Lift hill is the first – and usually highest – hill on a roller coaster. The drop from this height helps propel the cars through the rest of the ride.

Magnetic propulsion is powering an object forwards using magnets.

Magnets are metals that attract other metals; usually those that contain iron. *(see also electromagnet)*

Pivot is a point around which an object turns.

Poles are the opposite points on a magnet where the magnetic forces are strongest. *(see also magnets)*

Pulley is a simple machine. Rope pulled through a wheel lifts an object at the other end.

Ramp is a simple machine that is a slope raised at one end. Ramps make it easier to move or lower objects.

Repel is to push away or apart. It is the opposite of attract.

Rigid means stiff, unchanging in shape.

Weight is the pull of gravity on an object's mass.